This book is for Ron

Junk Mail

Michael Harrison

Oxford University Press
Oxford New York Toronto

Oxford University Press, Walton Street, Oxford OX2 6DP
Oxford New York Toronto
Delhi Bombay Calcutta Madras Karachi
Kuala Lumpur Singapore Hong Kong Tokyo
Nairobi Dar es Salaam Cape Town
Melbourne Auckland Madrid

and associated companies in
Berlin Ibadan

Oxford is a trade mark of Oxford University Press

First published 1993

ISBN 0 19 276107 2 (hardback)
ISBN 0 19 276113 7 (paperback)

A CIP catalogue record for this book is available from the British Library

Illustrated by Sue Heap

Printed in Great Britain on acid-free paper by
Biddles Ltd, Guildford and King's Lynn

Contents

Dear Miss Muffet,

Are your picnics spoilt by
– buzzings in your ear
– swoopings in your face
– fallings in your curds-and-whey?
In short: are you troubled by
F L I E S ?
Ours is a GREEN company.
We use only ecologically sound
Recycled webs.
Our representative
is close to you NOW
and looks forward to
sitting down with you
to discuss your needs.

The Rent-A-Spider Company plc

Dear Little Boy Blue,

Have you been under attack
recently?
Have there been complaints about
– modern farming methods
– noisy musical instruments
– lack of equal opportunities?

We are Image Revivers
to many public companies.
'Change the name
Stay the same!'
is our slogan.

May we suggest
GREEN GIRL plc ©
fits the modern world
more acceptably?

You could then securely sleep
Under your haycock, forgetting
sheep.

The White Washers.

Dear Mr Dumpty,

We are an American company
whose commemorative china
is eagerly sought after.

This Fall we are offering
a Collection of Eggcups
with the badges of the Great
Regiments
hand-painted on the sides.

Rush your order to us
before it is too late.

The Wallsend China Company

P.S. The first hundred applicants
will all receive, free of charge,
a tube of Super-glue, just in case.

Dear Prince Charming,

How many pairs of shoes
does a modern palace hold?
How much valuable time
is wasted cleaning them?

Our special team
moves in after midnight
and works while you sleep.

You need never worry
about shoes again.

Sarah and Jane Ugly –
The Fitter Foot Firm.

P.S. We have just started
a new service: windows
and glass slippers cleaned.
No order too small.

When Granny comes to stay
She brings her black handbag.
As soon as she's in through the door,
'Let me see what I've got here,'
She says.
She opens her bag
And in goes her hand
And out come my favourite sweets.

If I need a pencil to draw the cat,
If she needs scissors to cut my nails,
If I scrape my knee and need a plaster,
'Let me see what I've got here,'
She says.
She opens her bag
And in goes her hand
And out comes whatever I need.

At home her bag behaves itself
And nothing strange is ever let out.
But once Granny and I are off on a walk
Just anything can come out of that bag.

One hot afternoon we are in the park.
'I'm tired and I'm hot,' I say.
'Let me see what I've got here,'

She says.
She opens her bag
And in goes her hand
And out comes a cone of strawberry ice-cream.

Suddenly we hear a noise, a humming brown noise.
'Bees,' says Granny, 'a swarm of bees.'
'Let me see what I've got here,'
She says.

She opens her bag
But she doesn't put in her hand.
She holds it open and, with a noise
Like the bath emptying,
All the bees swarm in.
'There,' says Granny, and shuts her bag,
'Let's go home for a cup of tea.'

It was a long way home. 'What we need,'
I say, 'is a short cut.'
'Let me see what I've got here,'
She says.
She opens her bag
And puts it down on the pavement.
She takes hold of my hand, and then,
And then we are in a huge dark cave.
There's a slight buzzing sound
And a smell of honey. 'Come on!'
Says Granny. 'We'll be late for tea.'

We step out into the sunlight
And there we are outside home,
And in we go, in time for tea.
'Let me see what I've got here,'
She says.
She opens her bag
And in goes her hand
And out comes a jar of honey.

This Poem

This poem is made up
of 100 per cent recycled
words and, once read,
can be carefully
cut up and re-used.

Walking to the Moon

(It would take a reasonably fit walker 8½ years to walk to the moon)

Eight years —if you keep going.
The first bit's easy: straight on at
The top of the hill, bear right
As the moon swings round the sky.

You'll be OK once past the clouds.
Don't panic when chunks of moon
Fall off—they'll be back, and go,
More than a hundred times.

Just keep plodding on. Breathing
May become difficult: try not to.
And it will be cold, so keep moving.
And whatever happens, don't look down.

Walking on the Moon

When they landed first
they walked, bounced rather,
leaving footprints in the dust.

But what's there to walk
for, or to? It's like us on
Christmas Day. We walk

because we can't stay
still. We've travelled long
towards this day, and now

we've landed. Pause, and
look round: it's not exactly
what we dreamed—and

so we walk. What would
you do if, against all
likelihood, you stood

on the dusty moon and saw
blue earth? I bet you
too would bounce, or walk.

Walking In

It's walking in
that is so hard,
especially if
the door is
shut.

Turning the handle
turns their eyes:
they all watch
me, walking
in.

Wanted

**WANTED: PAPER
BOYS AND GIRLS**

So the notice said.

And who can blame them?
Think of the benefits
over slugs and snails,
or even,
sugar and spice.

Wanted (2)

Of course, the caring
politician says comfortably,
you must have the right
paper qualifications to
sleep in a cardboard box.

Proverb

In the eggs
the chickens say,
'Don't count
your foxes
before
you're hatched.'

Haircut

What I hate
about having a haircut
is being asked
how I want it
when I don't want it cut at all.

What I hate
about having a haircut
is being asked
questions with
the whole room listening to my answers.

What I hate
about having a haircut

is being asked
to look in
the mirror and say how I like it.

What I hate most
about having a haircut
is going to school
and everyone
telling me I've had my hair cut.

Dear Mouth Owner,

Do you have a mouth
you find hard to control?

Have you tried
will-power
Sellotape
sticky toffee
Polyfilla
unsuccessfully?

You haven't tried our
Mouth Obedience Classes.

After just one lesson
you will amaze your teachers.

Their mouths will fall open
as yours stays shut.

I Hate Teachers

I
hate
teachers
who
slowly
uncoil
their
tongues

before lashing angrily
at my ears
again and again and again.

They
pause
only
for
me
to
mumble
'yes'

before lapping greedily
at my tears
again and again and again.

Teachers Say

'It's like talking
to a brick wall.'
How do they know?
Do you learn
to be a teacher
standing in a line
facing a wall,
and just talk, talk?

Did Humpty fall
from boredom
at all this blah
beneath him?
My advice is:
'For bouncing off
use walls for balls;
ears need ideas.'

How to Recognize Rude Words

(from *The Alien's Guide*)

Words, of course, are noises
and so often rude, as are most
noises that the body makes.

Volume is important: quiet
is safest, but not whispered.

Some words are always rude.
These are mainly words about
bodies. (So much of body is
covered up, it's odd there are
words for some of it at all.)

Strangest of all are words
of dimension: a narrow mind
is bad, a fat body worse
but fighting can break out
if you call the earthling 'Thick'.

Liar

I am a liar, of course,
a story-teller, as all
writers are. It's my job.

What I'm telling you now
is the truth: you can't
believe a word I say.

Miss! Sue is Kissing

Miss! Sue is kissing
the tadpoles again.
She is, Miss. I did,
I asked her. She said
something about catching
him young. Getting one
her own age. I don't know,
Miss. She keeps whispering,
'Prince, Prince.' Isn't that
a dog's name, Miss?

Middle Child

The eldest son goes first
In all the stories. He makes
The mistakes we need
For an exciting beginning.

The youngest goes last,
Is kind to old women,
Feeds small creatures,
Wins the happy ending.

But the second son fails
In just the same ways:
The same rudeness, unkindness.
I just fill up the middle.

Parable with Moral

Socks get separated and lost left
In a drawer; one is no use. They
Must be worn together. So too
Our friends drift if left alone. We
Need companions to keep the heart warm.

Instruction Manual

I have lost the instructions
that came with me.
I know there were some
because my parents, teachers,
younger sister, told me
with such conviction
exactly what to do, and
how to do it.
                    But now that
there is no one to tell me,
I can't find the instructions.

Doing my Homework

Doing my homework last night
I ran out of time . . .
They don't seem to stock it
At our branch of Tesco.
I asked my mum if she
Could spare me a minute . . .
I said I'd bring it back
As soon as I'd finished.

Summer Time

What a waste it is
the clocks go forward,
losing a whole hour,
in the middle of the night.
Think of the day-time hours
we would be better without,
from school or dentist or
just waiting for time to pass.

And what a waste
to put the clocks back
one whole night hour
when there are so many
hours we could have again.
Who's in charge here, us or time?

Diary

Got up, went to school,
did homework, went to bed.

All that is net: life's
quick fish escaped.

On the Beach

The waves claw
At the shingle
Time after time.
They fall back
Again and again,
Sighing, sighing.

Island

You pause here, on the island's edge
Where the shallow sea tugs your feet.
You feel uneasy, that you're being watched.
You see yourself stand uncertain
In the wet sand's rippled mirror—
But it's more than that. You step
Silently forward, leaving no footprints
Behind you as the sea sweeps after you.
You glance uneasily around you,
Look back over your shoulder: land,
Sea stare empty back. The feeling
Grows: there are eyes on this island.

Stone Haiku

These haiku are meant to be written on stones brought home from the beach. You can spiral the writing around or arrange it to fit the stone. Write the place and date you found the stone on the underneath. Write in felt-tip and then varnish the stone to make it shiny.

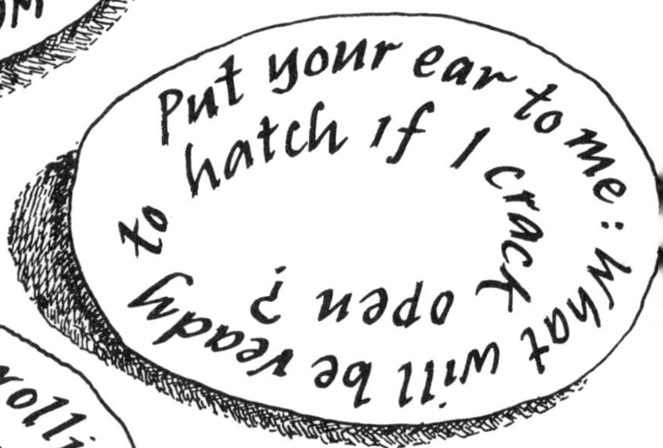

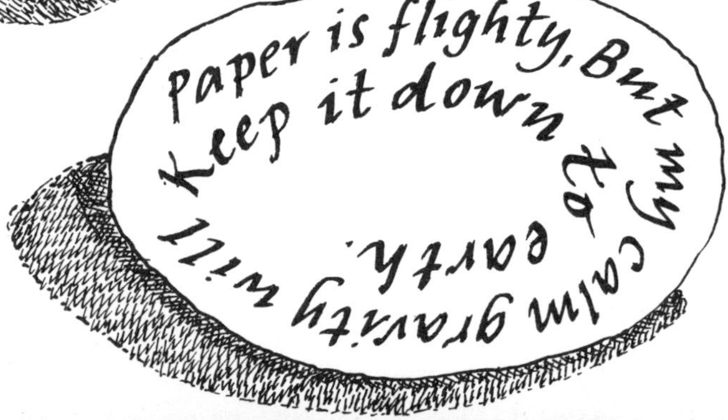

Books

Books don't face you
fluttering their pages.
They sit, spines out,
their titles edging
nervously sideways.

Take one in hand,
open it gently.
It will pull you
out of this square-
edged world into

its private mazed ways.
Beware: you are booked.
Escape is not easy,
especially for those
who are happily hooked.

No Right Turn

NO RIGHT TURN

the sign said.

Can you wonder
that we're lost?

Scaffolding

It is
too easy to say it is a spider's web.
It has none of the spiralling sagginess,
the lightness concealing deadly purpose.
Nor does it appear silently overnight
but comes and goes with clattering conceit.
In between, it sits there all up-tight.

It is
more like a play-pen
behind whose bars the house
sulks out of baleful windows.

It is
more like a climbing-frame
where the house lurks nervously
for fear of playground bullies.

It is
more like a supermarket trolley
abandoned in the bushes
which has filled up with bricks.

It is
more like a space-ship's gantry
for user-friendly moon-trips
'in the comfort of your own home'.

Quite simply, it is the perfect present
for those who have out-grown Lego.

Spider

Glittering through the sky
Insects land safely
At scarlet supermarkets,
The shelves stacked with nectar.

My food flies off.
I cannot soar after
But must scuttle through
The dead leaves.

Out of my abdomen
I spin sticky ropes—
Fill the green freeways
With my shopping trolley.

Penguin

('The male penguin . . . picks up a pebble in his bill, waddles over to a bird standing alone and solemnly lays it before it . . . if the stranger receives the pebble with a deep bow then he has discovered his true mate.' David Attenborough: *Life on Earth*)

This stone I set at your feet
As my courtship gift to you
At the white summer's end
On Antarctica's icy shore.

Later you lay your egg
And ease it on to my feet.
You turn and walk away,
Black going into the blackness.

I stand, Emperor of this land,
My back to the blistering wind,
Shifting my feet with care
Through the dark of sixty days.

Will you return as the egg hatches,
Fat, and with belly full to feed
Our young? Will you find us here
Amidst this blinding snow?

Yes, and I must now walk
My shrunken self the hundred icy
Miles to open sea, then, fattened,
The hundred back, my belly lardered.

And so through all the long dark
We trudge, or stand, under the howling sky.
In the fading summer I will bring again
The honest gift of a stone.

Windows

From the speeding train window,
From the still bedroom window,
Our glances meet: one
Moment and then gone.
We do not even raise our hands
To wing us apart.

Will this eye-collision repeat
Next time train passes window?

when they get the chance
jump on to women's wrists
and cling there, tugging
them towards the shops.

Why? They like to fetch
their fatter cousins home:
carrier-bags with swollen
omnivorous bellies.

Men, the weaker sex,
have for their parasites
the lighter wallet, which,
Roo-like, prefers a pocket.

Dead End

My job? Well, I write
street names. No, not
the actual metal plates.
I make up the names.
Yes, it's interesting
and trickier than you'd think.
To start with, no one wants
them funny, or hard to say,
or spell. You know, the
embarrassment in shops.
And they end in such
limited ways: street, road.
No, I've not had one used yet.
It takes time to make your name.

Weathers

Weathers are moody:
Hyperactive Wind
is never still;
Wet Fog
just hangs around;
Ebullient Hail
bounces back.

Rain doesn't muck about:
he's down to earth.

Snow

Through the classroom window we watch the
snow fall.
We have to write a poem, of course. We've done
Wind and clouds and rain. So now snow.
What is there new to say? Under the microscope
Each flake is different, and each of us
Is easily distinguished by the casual eye—but
Our poems will lie, identical corpses on white
sheets.
Our hands can hold it a little time, grow cold too,
But snow's sudden shock melts in the warmth of
words.

An Anglo-Saxon Riddle Turned into a Haiku

On my winter walk
I see a riddle. Look there!
Water turned to bone.

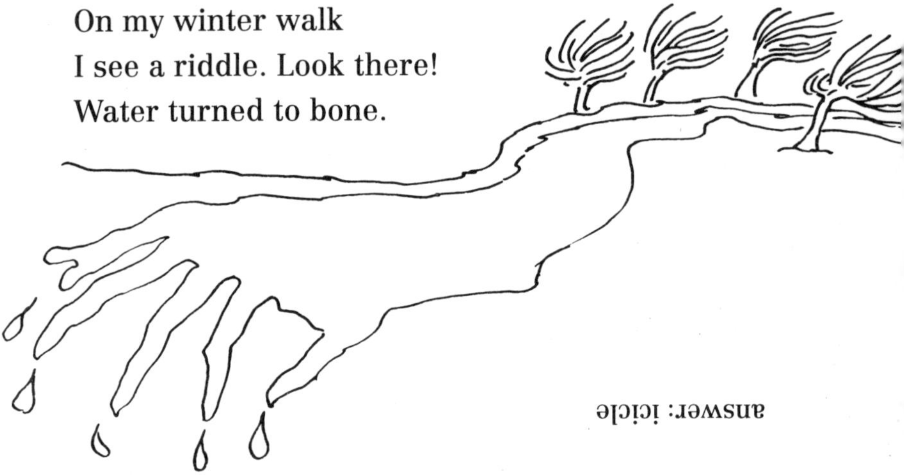

answer: icicle

Spring

Spring
slips
silent
snowdrops
past Winter's iron gate.

Then daffodils'
golden trumpets
sound:
Victory!

Butterfly

Butterfly
Butterflies
Butterflown

Monday

Moon's Day: the first day
Ought to shine in the week like
New minted silver.

Dull copper thoughts just
Add another penny to
Yesterday's small change.

Toms 80p

For a moment I see their faces
piled up: all the Toms I have known.

Some I would gladly have paid
to have had taken off my hands.

But others I remember now fondly:
each separate Tom's face, sharp, fresh.

Then raw reality rolls back:
comatose, supermarket-bland, tomatoes.

Exhausted

I'm exhausted,
she said. My trouble
is, I can't remember
ever being hausted.

The Sower

Listen!
A sower went out to sow.
Wait a moment. You have
the wrong picture in your mind.
This is not a man on a tractor,
glass cab to keep out the weather,
Walkman on his ears,
wheels and gears and clatter
behind him, and straight lines
of covered seed, exactly placed.
Farming for the supermarket shelves:
golden harvest for yellow Weetabix boxes.

No, not like that at all. Listen!

A sower went out to sow.
His feet walking the unsteady earth,
wind, sun, shower touching him,
bird cries in his ears. His basket
of seed bumping his belly
at every stride. Hands left, right,
left, right: into the basket, clutch
the seed, cast. Keeping a steady pace;
counting: one, two, three, four: throw.
To each grain its little piece of earth,
its tiny grave. A sower went out.

Picture the grains of wheat
lying in the basket.
Hand comes down
grasps,
lifts,
casts.
Arc through the air;
fall to the ground.
Where do they land?

Some—
thrown a little hard,
carried by the wind,
lighter than the rest—
land on the path.
The crying, squabbling
birds swoop, peck,
and are fed.

Some
go further still,
into the thorn bushes.
Thorn roots tug water
from the soil; thorn
leaves catch the sun.
The wheat grows pale,
weedy, fruitless.

Some
lands on stony ground.
It swells, roots creep
through the earth until
BLOCKED:
no space
no depth
no moisture.
As the golden sun
climbs up the sky
calling water to him,
these

sag,
wilt,
frizzle,
die.

What can we harvest
this summer?
What can we eat
this winter?
What bread can we bake?
Our wheat is
stolen,
choked,
wilted.

Listen!
Those grains are the mistakes.
The sower strides down the field,
casts broad sweeps, left, right,
left,
right.
Seed falls in rich soil.
Roots tunnel greedily,
leaves soak up the sun,
grain swells,
ripens,
goldens,
waits for the harvesters' hands.
Each seed turns into a hundred.

Ground, baked
into our bread.

Listen!
Let these words
fall into your hearts
like seed into the good earth
and then you will bear
good seed
a hundredfold.

Adam Speaks

I should have said:

Your Eden is a zoo,
us the exhibits for
the cool of your day.
Out here, OK, it's no
paradise, but it is
a whole new world.

I should have said:

The woman gave me
to eat, thank God.

1: Prodigal Son

Better put on a bit of a show;
The old man will like that.
The real hurt is buried inside:
After the feast, tomorrow,
Back in the fields, grubbing about,
Knowing now there's no escape.

2: Brother

Better put on a bit of a sulk
Though really I'm glad he's back.
No one talked about him. We
Stepped over the gaps, closed
The spaces he had left. It was dull:
Just work, and silence.

3: Mother

These men, acting their parts:
Gestures larger than life—repentence,
Forgiveness, jealousy—to draw all
The attention away from their pain.
My daughters make no fuss, and I,
I have disappeared from the story.

Before Christmas

The year tips, the sun
slips towards the sky's edge, and
dark bites at the day.

Shopping after dark:
hands clutching carrier-bags
stuffed with surprises.

The pillar-box's
smiling mouth swallows our cards,
cheered by the greetings.

Christmas cards snow through
the letter-box. Open them
and brightness thaws out.

Lying awake I
hear clattering hooves: reindeer
landing on the roof.

What is Christmas?

Christmas is a lighted island
In the sea of winter darkness.

Christmas is the reindeer clatter
On the roof of the rustling house.

Christmas is the spiced kitchen
Spreading through the waiting days.

Christmas is the tongue teased
And the tummy truly tested.

Christmas is the warm hug
That wraps me in my family's love.

In the Stable: Christmas Haiku

Donkey
My long ears can hear
Angels singing, but my song
Would wake the baby.

Dog
I will not bark but
Lie, head on paws, eyes watching
All these visitors.

Cat
I will wash my feet. For
This baby all should be clean.
My purr will soothe him.

Owl
My round eyes look down.
No starlit hunting this night:
Peace to little ones!

Spider
My fine web sparkles:
Indoor star in the roof's night
Over the baby.

After Christmas

Darkness begins a
retreat: the cold light flows back
over the dead land.

Put the tree out: hang
nuts on its branches—feathered
decorations come.

Take down the Christmas
cards: arrowheads in the dust
point to spring cleaning.

Pull down the paper
chains: the room grows tall, the floor
deep in coloured snow.

Cold bites deep: warm your
mind at Christmas memories
and look for snowdrops.

Thomas

I can hide here in the reeds;
They are never still or quiet.

They have taken my mother;
They say she is a witch.

Damp seeps up from the marsh;
There is nothing firm under me.

They say she is a witch;
And they came to take me too.

Darkness creeps through the reeds
And laps at the sky's blood.

And they came to take me too
So that I could speak against her.

There are noises around me;
They are rustling closer and closer.

So that I could speak against her
And tell of her cats and her herbs.

I want my mother to hold me;
I want her to keep me safe.

Because of her cats and her herbs
They have taken my mother.

Thomas was aged eight when his mother, Ursula Kemp, was hanged as a witch. He was questioned at her trial at St Osyth's, Essex.

Child in Hospital

sleeping child, the
growing brambles
are inside you

what cruel god-
mother wished this
ten years ago?

from the window
through the glass
lightly the city lies

I speak your name
your hand creeps out
to slow the widening

void

Brass Rubbing

Rubbing black wax on white paper:
The faces of the stately dead rise
Out of the clearly ordered past.

Above, a stone plaque, casually glimpsed,
Then its cut letters tear my eyes:
'Aged six months and twelve days.'

Those twelve days!

Sunday Fathers

I used to notice them,
one of the Sunday sights:
fathers visiting their children
and walking them in parks
or sitting over milk-shakes
making careful conversation.

I saw a pair one Sunday
looking in a shop window,
I thought, but the boy's eyes

were curtained with tears
and the father's arms were shut
out by more than the week.

Now I try not to see them:
such a shadow on the sun's day

The Somme Battlefield

At dawn we walked the few yards
From the front line to where they fell.
Crossing the stubble I bent and picked up
Bullets that had been earthed seventy years.

Later we met an old woman
Weeding in the village cemetery.
'This is my grave, just here, beside my husband,'
And she patted the patient waiting earth—

This same earth that takes them all:
The torn lives, and the rounded ones.
In the July sun larks sing over the red poppies
And the soldiers' white stones, like bleached
bones.

Harlech Castle

Here, decayed, an old
Giant's molar. It ground men's
Bones; their blood its bread.

In Chichester Cathedral

The stone smells cold and hard. Through the
  round arch
A pillar struts, then spreads out. By it
Black iron railings, the uprights ending
With spear heads, pen in a white tomb—feet at
Ease on a marble cushion. On the wall behind
Extravagant words bring a brief immortality.

Stone mocks our aspiration and our love:
Beneath my feet lie rows of erased names.

The rush-bottomed chairs wait
For the faithful, but people wander,
Hands uneasily casual in pockets, looking
For some talking point, wondering why
They will leave unchanged.
The stone's a riddle we can't solve.

The Quarry at Ancaster

At dusk we dropped down into the quarry.
It was silent, shadowed. Piles of smashed rock
Gloomed up. Our heads touched as we looked
  along
The slabbed wall for fossils in the torch-light.

A motor-bike drilling the night stopped.
Silence. We stood close in darkness, waiting.
It roared to life, went. Whispers close to hair.
The stones slipped and chinked beneath our feet.

Stubble burned in the fields. We walked across
And stood holding hands, soft ash underfoot,
Silently looking at the red glow, the
Flickering flame, and smoke across the moon.

Sleeping Beauty: The Prince Hesitates

Tangled thickets of thorn and bramble:
Bend down and see tracks—
Animals on undisturbed errands
Wearing away the placid grass.

To press through is to risk eyes
Crying bloodily in a face
Patterned with red beads,
Clothes gasping to blue air,
Heart laid open, torn,
While dusk thickens and owls hoot.

Sleeping Beauty Awake

I used to think that Sleeping Beauty
Might not wake with gladness, might
Dislike her prince, his bland certainty,
All the consequences of the kiss:
The endless washing up, the nappies,
And sponsor forms from school.
Sleep might seem the better choice.
Now I know that thorns that tear
Are better in the hand than dreams.

To Sail a Thin Boat

To sail a thin boat through the heavy wind
over quaking water is an image
of what we would like our living to be.

Each part has its job and can be tested:
the plastic bucket is tied to the mast,
the jib-sheets end with a figure-of-eight.

I went out with a girl once, in a boat.
She helmed, I crewed, throwing my weight about,
straining my body to balance the boat.

We rushed up the harbour at such angles
that the grey stable world was sliced open
and yearning tongues licked up the boat at us.

If you capsize, the instructor had said,
never leave your boat. Other dry advice
was given. It works. We tried it that day.

But the emotions cannot be tamed so.

Bridge

I pause when I reach
this bridge and look down
into the water's separate world.
Above me swifts chase oblivious
flies. Harder is to pause
in time: the past flowing
liquidly away, the future
open-beaked, approaching.

By-Pass

The cars slide across the fields of childhood.
Behind them, green meadows, fringing willows,
Evening's standard sky and uncertain black birds.

I hold a photo that shows time by-passed:
My boy's body in the same river,
Face looking back into my older eyes.

We have travelled far, he and I.
Now the upright fence separates me from
The fields that were and the road that is.

Country Road

The summer road is neatly laid
With this day's harvest of corpses,
Some only too identifiable—
Eyes still glaring incredulity—
Others are pancaked to passivity
Or beef-burgered into anonymity
By the uncaring cars' urgent appetites.

They feed on life: these bodies are the price.

The End of the World

Let us think, just for a moment,
about the end of the world.

It used to be so simple: it was
them, the politicians, their fingers
on the button that would reduce us,
us their innocent offerings, to ash.

But now, now it is not so easy.
Now it is me, with my fingers
on my ignition key, moving
my car closer to the end of the world.

Now it is me. My fingers are the hand
of God, making the waters rise, my car
the ark of destruction which leaves
rainbows behind it, in oil on the road.

Junk Male

Dear Male Reader,

Are you often embarrassed
at being a man?
Do you shudder at the way
men have behaved, that they
have invented weapons of destruction
and started wars to use them:
tortured, shot, gassed, bombed
their way through his-story
and now booze and brawl
through their tabloid world
as if they were lords
of the Devil's creation?

Do you cringe to know
that women fear you,
that our very world
is dying at men's hands?

Is your greatest longing
for man to be remade?
Would you like to be free
to cry and be comforted,

to wrap your arms around your friends,
to be turned to by children in pain,

without fear of the harsh taunts
that mean you are no man?

Would you like to shape
a history to be proud of?

Well, tough . . .